Published in 2025 by Groundwood Books / House of Anansi Press
groundwoodbooks.com

We gratefully acknowledge for their financial support of our publishing program the Canada Council for the Arts, the Ontario Arts Council and the Government of Canada.

Canada Council for the Arts   Conseil des Art du Canada

ONTARIO ARTS COUNCIL
CONSEIL DES ARTS DE L'ONTARIO
an Ontario government agency
un organisme du gouvernement de l'Ontario

With the participation of the Government of Canada
Avec la participation du gouvernement du Canada   Canadä

Library and Archives Canada Cataloguing in Publication

Title: Cats and us : a ten-thousand-year fascination / written and illustrated by Marta Pantaleo ; translated by Debbie Bibo & Yvette Ghione.
Other titles: I gatti e noi. English
Names: Pantaleo, Marta, author, illustrator. | Bibo, Debbie, translator. | Ghione, Yvette, translator.
Description: Translation of: I gatti e noi : storia di un legame lungo 10.000 anni | In English, translated from the Italian.
Identifiers: Canadiana (print) 20240528557 | Canadiana (ebook) 20240530179 | ISBN 9781779460394 (hardcover) | ISBN 9781779460417 (Kindle) | ISBN 9781779460400 (EPUB)
Subjects: LCSH: Cats—Juvenile literature. | LCSH: Cats—History—Juvenile literature. | LCSH: Human-animal relationships—Juvenile literature. | LCGFT: Informational works. | LCGFT: Picture books.
Classification: LCC SF442 .P3613 2025 | DDC j636.8—dc23

The illustrations were created digitally.
Edited by Samantha Dewaele
Designed by Marta Pantaleo
Printed and bound in China

FSC
www.fsc.org
MIX
Paper | Supporting responsible forestry
FSC® C008047

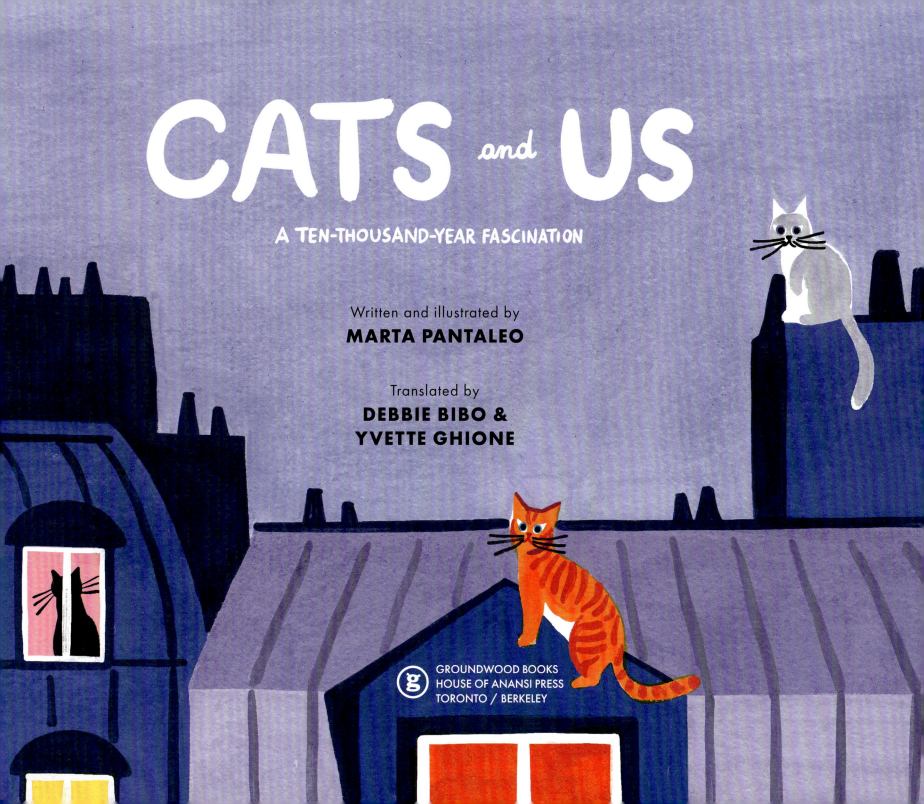

CATS and US

A TEN-THOUSAND-YEAR FASCINATION

Written and illustrated by
MARTA PANTALEO

Translated by
**DEBBIE BIBO &
YVETTE GHIONE**

GROUNDWOOD BOOKS
HOUSE OF ANANSI PRESS
TORONTO / BERKELEY

The mysterious nature of cats has always intrigued us.

It's been this way since ancient times,

when there were no big cities, and wild cats lived alongside people in the wilderness.

They were unafraid of the dark, and their striped fur helped them hide at night.

Quick and stealthy, their hunting helped farmers keep pests away.

We admired and revered them,

and they became
our close companions.

We took them with us on our journeys.

They knew how to spot even the smallest, most unwelcome guest!

And so they traveled to every corner of the world.

They gave rise to myths,

legends,

superstitions,

and heroic tales.

They kept their old habits,

and managed to learn new ones.

Over the centuries, they taught us their language,

and today we can understand each other.

But just when we think we know everything about them ...

... they can seem incomprehensible

and bizarre to us.

It isn't easy to figure out what is really going on in their heads.

They are full of secrets that they keep only for themselves.

But when they reveal one to us ...

... they make us feel special.

HERE ARE SOME OF THE MOST POPULAR CAT BREEDS!
Can you find them in the book?

PERSIAN Originated in Asia Minor. Its long, fluffy coat, which can grow up to eight inches (twenty centimeters) long, gives this elegant breed a regal bearing.

BIRMAN In Ancient Burma (Myanmar today), these cats served as Buddhist temple guardians, and the breed became known as "the sacred cat." Their eyes are blue, and their paws are always pure white.

NORWEGIAN FOREST CAT A large, robust breed originating in the forests of Norway. This bushy-tailed cat often appears in Norwegian myths pulling a chariot for the goddess Freya.

TURKISH ANGORA Originated in Anatolia (central Turkey today). Centuries ago, sultans of the Ottoman Empire sent these elegant, silky-coated cats as gifts to the English and French royal courts.

SIBERIAN Originated in Russia. Has a sturdy build and a thick coat with long, luxurious fur perfect for keeping it warm during freezing winters.

BALINESE A longer-haired variation of the Siamese, first bred in the 1940s. Lively and affectionate, it has a full, plumed tail, and its silky coat hugs its body.

AMERICAN CURL A highly intelligent, affectionate and playful breed. Its ears are its most distinctive feature: wide set and backward curling. They look like rosebuds when the cats are young kittens.

MAINE COON One of the largest of all domestic cat breed Has a powerful, muscular body with a thick, shaggy coat and distinctive tuft-tipped ears.

RAGDOLL A solid, muscular breed with a large head and deep blue eyes. These cats are named for the way they go completely limp when held.

Cats can be grouped into three categories, according to the length of their fur.

OMALI A highly curious breed that eagerly follows its owners. Their sleek bodies, long tails and large pointed ears have earned them the nickname of "fox cat."

YORK CHOCOLATE A large breed with a soft, distinctive chocolate-brown coat. These cats have a sweet and lively character.

TURKISH VAN An ancient breed known in Turkey as "the swimming cat" for its love of water. It is white in color with darker markings on its head and tail. In winter its coat is thick and soft like cashmere.

SHORT-HAIRED BREEDS

Most of the cats we know today are short-haired cats!

ENGAL A cross between the domestic cat and the wild sian leopard cat, this spotted breed was created in the 1960s. is one of the few breeds that enjoys water.

CHARTREUX Dates back to the Middle Ages and is thought to be named for Carthusian monks in France who might have kept them as mousers. Has pumpkin-colored eyes, a sturdy build and a pure blue coat.

CORNISH REX All cats of this breed are related to the first naturally curly-haired kitten that was born on a farm in Cornwall, England, in the 1950s. Even the whiskers on these cats are curly!

EXOTIC SHORTHAIR A robust, medium-sized breed. Its head is large and round, with small, low-set ears and a flat face. Its coat may be any combination of colors and patterns.

FOREIGN WHITE First bred in the 1960s. A cross between the Siamese and the white domestic cat, it has a distinctive pure white coat. These delicate cats bond closely with their owners.

CEYLON Originated in Sri Lanka, where it had evolved naturally. One of very few natural breeds to be officially recognized.

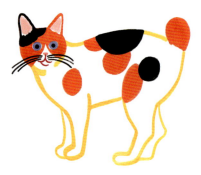

JAPANESE BOBTAIL Originating in Japan, this curious and intelligent breed is revered for bringing good luck. It has a muscular body and a pom-pom tail.

ORIENTAL SHORTHAIR First bred in Great Britain in the 1950s. Has a slender body and large ears, and its coat can be long-haired or short-haired. Lively and chatty, these cats are very attached to their owners.

EUROPEAN SHORTHAIR Originating in Europe, this breed's coat can be a variety of colors and patterns. These cats are independent but affectionate.

SCOTTISH FOLD Originating in Scotland, this cat is known for the shape of its ears, which are folded down toward the front of the head.

SIAMESE Originating in Thailand, it is one of the oldest breeds. It is known for its characteristic triangle-shaped head, large ears and blue eyes. These cats have a lively temperament.

SINGAPURA Originating in Singapore, the smallest of the domestic cats! Playful, affectionate and curious, these cats are very attached to the members of their family.

BRITISH SHORTHAIR From Great Britain, descended directly from cats brought from Ancient Rome. An affectionate breed, it has a sturdy body and round head, and its coat is as soft as a plush toy.

THAI Close in appearance and character to the Siamese, but calmer in temperament. Affectionate and social, these cats are very vocal — they love to chat with their owners!

TONKINESE A cross between the Siamese and Burmese, first bred in the 1960s. It has a slender, muscular body and almond-shaped blue-green eyes. These intelligent cats enjoy family life.

ABYSSINIAN Once kept by Egyptian pharaohs, this may be the oldest cat breed of all! Muscular and agile, it has a wedge-shaped head, and its coat often bears ticked markings.

OCICAT First bred in the United States by crossing the Abyssinian, Siamese and American shorthair. Its spotted coat makes it look similar to a wild ocelot, but this breed loves to interact with people.

RUSSIAN BLUE Dates from the end of the nineteenth century in Russia. Has a long and elegant body and a blue-gray coat with a silvery sheen. These cats are very shy with strangers.

BURMILLA Accidentally first bred in Great Britain in the 1980s through the crossing of the Burmese and the Chinchilla Persian. It has a soft coat with a silvery sheen and appears to be wearing eyeliner!

EGYPTIAN MAU "Mau" comes from the ancient Egyptian word for "cat." Its hind legs are especially long, and its coat has a natural spotted pattern. These cats are lively and intelligent.

HAVANA BROWN First bred in the 1950s by crossing the Siamese with the common black cat, it is an elegant breed known for its mahogany coloring. These cats are especially curious.

MANX Dating from the end of the nineteenth century, this breed originates in the Isle of Man. It is characterized by the total or partial absence of a tail.

BOMBAY First bred in the United States in the 1950s. Though its short, shiny, all-black coat gives it the mysterious air of a roaming panther, it is definitely an indoor cat.

SPHYNX The most unusual breed! Its muscular body is nearly hairless, with wrinkled skin and very fine down the texture of peach skin. These cats require extra-special care.